The Fact-Packed ACTIVITY Book

DINOSAURS

Editors Katie Lawrence, Niharika Prabhakar
Senior Editor Roohi Sehgal
US Editor Mindy Fichter
US Senior Editor Shannon Beatty
Project Art Editor Roohi Rais
Art Editors Bettina Myklebust Stovne,
Bhagyashree Nayak, Mohd Zishan
Assistant Art Editor Simran Lakhiani
Publishing Co-ordinator Issy Walsh
Jacket Designer Alison Tutton
DTP Designer Dheeraj Singh, Syed Md Farhan
Project Picture Researcher Sakshi Saluja
Senior Production Editors Robert Dunn, Nikoleta Parasaki
Production Controller Magdalena Bojko
Managing Editors Laura Gilbert, Monica Saigal
Managing Art Editors Diane Peyton Jones,
Ivy Sengupta
Delhi Creative Heads Glenda Fernandes,
Malavika Talukder
Publishing Manager Francesca Young
Deputy Art Director Mabel Chan
Publishing Director Sarah Larter

Consultants Dr. Dean Lomax, Emily Keeble

Material in this publication was previously published in:
Ultimate Factivity Collection Dinosaurs (2014)

First American Edition, 2022
Published in the United States by DK Publishing
1450 Broadway, Suite 801, New York, NY 10018

Copyright © 2022 Dorling Kindersley Limited
DK, a Division of Penguin Random House LLC
22 23 24 25 26 10 9 8 7 6 5 4 3 2 1
001–327000–May/2022

A catalog record for this book is available from the
Library of Congress.
ISBN: 978-0-7440-5155-1

DK books are available at special discounts when purchased
in bulk for sales promotions, premiums, fund-raising, or educational
use. For details, contact: DK Publishing Special Markets,
1450 Broadway, Suite 801, New York, NY 10018
SpecialSales@dk.com

Printed and bound in China

For the curious
www.dk.com

Contents

How this book works

Here is some information to help you find your way around this book, which is all about dinosaurs and other prehistoric animals.

These boxes give some fun facts about a topic.

Activities

There are many exciting activities for you to do in this book. All you need are a pen or pencil, crayons, a little imagination, and a thirst for knowledge!

Look for this roundel on every spread. It tells you what the activity is.

MATCH

the descriptions to each dinosaur. Check your answers on pp. 92–93.

Answers

The answers to all the questions are on pp. 92–93. Good luck!

Instructions

All of the instructions you'll need to complete an activity can be found on each page.

Play and Learn

Read and Create

Draw and Learn

Fact Challenge

Match and Learn

Look and Find

Test Your Knowledge

These are the different types of activities that you will find in the book:

1 **Play and Learn:** Follow the lines or join the dots to discover more about dinosaurs.

2 **Read and Create:** After reading the pages, use your markers or colored pencils to color the pictures.

3 **Draw and Learn:** Get ready with your pencils to draw, learn, and have fun.

4 **Fact Challenge:** Play a game and learn some fascinating facts.

5 **Match and Learn:** Match the descriptions with the pictures.

6 **Look and Find:** Let's see how well you can spot the pictures in the book.

7 **Test Your Knowledge:** Test yourself by answering mind-boggling questions.

Amazing activities will help you understand a specific topic better.

Introductions give you an overview of the topic that is being discussed on the pages.

5

The prehistoric world

Long ago, before humans ever existed, amazing creatures called dinosaurs roamed the Earth. These incredible reptiles are some of history's greatest treasures.

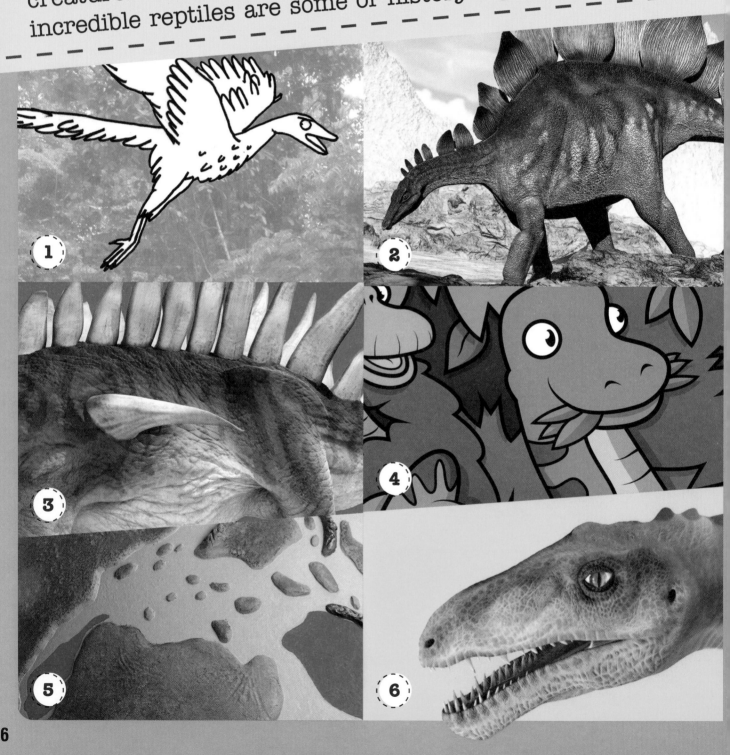

1

2

3

4

5

6

FIND
where these pictures are on pp. 8–29. Check your answers on pp. 92–93.

7

8

9

10

11

12

What did they look like?

Big, small, and everything in between, dinosaurs came in all shapes and sizes.

Stegosaurus

- Walked on all fours, low to the ground.
- Had short front legs and longer back legs with hoof-like toes.
- A double row of diamond-shaped plates ran down its neck, back, and long tail.
- Its head was narrow with a beak-like mouth.

SIZE GUIDE

1 What shape were the plates on Stegosaurus's back?

2 How many horns did Triceratops have?

Triceratops

- Walked on all fours with short, thick legs.
- Had a large, bony frill that looked like a collar covering its neck.
- Had two large horns above its eyes and a smaller one by its nose.
- It had a rhino-like body.

SIZE GUIDE

Eoraptor

- Walked and ran on its strong back legs.
- It wasn't much bigger than a chicken, but had a large head.
- Had sharp claws.

SIZE GUIDE

3 — What bird was Eoraptor close to in size?

FIND
the answers to these questions. Check your answers on pp. 92–93.

Brachiosaurus

- Its gigantic body was supported by thick, strong legs.
- A very long neck helped it reach treetops for food.
- Had a very long and thick tail.
- Its head was small for its size, with a bump on top.

SIZE GUIDE

Can you find all these dinosaurs in this book?

4 — What helped Brachiosaurus reach treetops for food?

The Mesozoic Era

COLOR
the dinosaurs and prehistoric creatures for all three periods of the Mesozoic Era.

Dinosaurs are one of the most successful creatures to ever exist. They ruled the Earth for around 170 million years during a time called the Mesozoic Era.

The Mesozoic Era is split up into three periods.

Pangaea

At the start of the Mesozoic Era, Earth's continents were all joined together into one big land mass called **Pangaea**, which means "All Earth." Over millions of years, the land broke up to form the continents we know today.

TRUE OR FALSE?
TYRANNOSAURUS LIVED CLOSER IN TIME TO HUMANS THAN IT DID TO TRIASSIC DINOSAURS.

Herrerasaurus

Coelophysis

Lesothosaurus

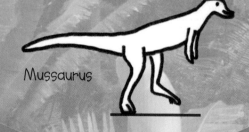

Mussaurus

Triassic period
252–201 million years ago

Pterodactylus

Archaeopteryx

Oviraptor

Brachiosaurus

Tyrannosaurus

Velociraptor

Stegosaurus

Triceratops

Pachycephalosaurus

Iguanodon

Spinosaurus

Cretaceous period
145–66 million years ago

Jurassic period
201–145 million years ago

Humans don't arrive
for millions of years!

11

The first dinosaurs

Plateosaurus

PLATE-ee-oh-SORE-us

At 25 ft (8 m) long, Plateosaurus was one of the biggest dinosaurs from the Triassic period.

Herrerasaurus

Her-RARE-uh-SORE-us

This early meat-eater lived 231 million years ago, but was only discovered in 1958.

Thecodontosaurus

THEE-co-DON-toe-SORE-us

One of the first dinosaurs to be discovered, its name means "socket-tooth lizard."

Pisanosaurus

PIH-san-uh-SORE-us

At only 3 ft (1 m) long, Pisanosaurus was one of the earliest known dinosaurs with bird-like hips.

Eoraptor

EE-oh-rap-tor

Around the size of a fox, Eoraptor used its sharp claws and teeth to help catch its prey.

These dinosaurs wouldn't have lived together in real life!

Triassic
period

SPOT these five dinosaurs in this scene. How many of each can you see?

The first period in the Mesozoic Era was called the Triassic. It spanned from 252–201 million years ago, and was the time when the first dinosaurs emerged.

Dinosaurs weren't very big during the Triassic period.

Check your answers on pp. 92–93.

TRUE OR FALSE?
THE DINOSAUR STEGOSAURUS LIVED DURING THE TRIASSIC PERIOD.

Facts about...

The Earth
Our planet looked very different during the Triassic period. Because it was so much **hotter and drier**, there weren't many plants, and most of the land was covered in desert.

13

Jurassic period

During the Jurassic period the planet became a lot cooler. This allowed more trees and plants to grow, and was one of the reasons so many new species of dinosaurs appeared.

FIND the five differences between the two pictures of the sauropods.

Sauropods like me are the biggest creatures to ever walk on land!

Brachiosaurus, one of the largest sauropods, grew to up to 75 ft (23 m) long!

Facts about...

Sauropods

These dinosaurs emerged during the late Triassic period. Many were giants with **long tails and necks**, which helped them reach leaves to eat from the tops of tall trees.

15

Cretaceous period

The Cretaceous period lasted for around 80 million years. By the time it was over, the Earth had become a very different place from the early days of the Triassic period.

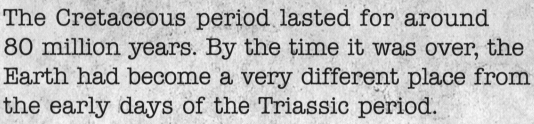

Triassic Earth

Toward the end of the Triassic period, the supercontinent Pangaea began to break up into several smaller landmasses.

Sauroposeidon

Pentaceratops

Giganotosaurus

Jurassic Earth

The newly formed continents drifted apart during the Jurassic period, creating large shallow seas.

FIND the answers to the questions. Check your answers on pp. 92–93.

Cretaceous Earth

During the Cretaceous period, the supercontinent Pangaea split farther apart and the Earth's continents began to look more like they do today.

I wonder what the world was like during the Cretaceous period.

Modern Earth

Today the Earth is divided into seven continents. They're still moving—it just happens so slowly that it's hard to tell.

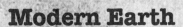

Gallimimus

Spinosaurus

Quiz

1 When did the supercontinent Pangaea begin to break up?

2 How long did the Cretaceous period last?

3 Can you figure out on which continent Spinosaurus lived?

Minmi

I lived in what is now North America. Can you tell where that was?

Different types of dinosaurs

Which type am I?

Saurischians
(SORE-is-kee-uns)

One type of dinosaurs, saurischians, were called "lizard-hipped."

An example of a saurischian's hip.

Theropods
(THERRO-pods)

A group of mostly meat-eaters that **walked on two legs**, theropods had strong jaws and curved teeth to help them chew meat.

Sauropodomorphs
(SORE-oh-POD-oh-morfs)

This group of plant-eaters had very **long necks and tails**, and were the biggest animals to ever walk the Earth.

Thyreophorans
(THIGH-ree-OFF-oh-rans)

These plant-eaters were famous for having impressive **armored plates** and spikes.

Ornithischians
(OR-nith-is-kee-uns)

The other type of dinosaurs, ornithischians, were called "bird-hipped."

An example of an ornithischian's hip.

Ornithopods
(OR-nith-oh-pods)

A very common group of dinosaurs, ornithopods reached for food with their **beaks and sharp teeth**.

Marginocephalians
(MAR-jee-no-sa-FAY-lee-ans)

Famous for their **frills and horns**, this group of plant-eaters were common during the Cretaceous period.

Dinosaurs

18

Dinosaurs came in all shapes and sizes, but there were only two main types (based on their hip bones). These dinosaurs could then be split up into five major groups.

Ouranosaurus

FOLLOW the lines to see which type of dinosaur each one is.

Huayangosaurus

Argentinosaurus

Triceratops

Wow, such amazing names!

Timimus

Count the
theropods

Theropods are a varied group of dinosaurs. Three different theropods have been let loose here. Can you count how many there are of each?

Coelophysis

Facts about...

Coelophysis
Coelophysis was a lightly built predator, weighing around 40–50 lb (18–23 kg). It had more than **100 small, sharp teeth** in its narrow jaws.

Allosaurus

Facts about...

The name Allosaurus means "different lizard." Armed with powerful legs, deadly claws, and sharp teeth—it was one of the **fiercest predators** in the Jurassic period.

Allosaurus

Ceratosaurus

Facts about...

This dinosaur had **three horns**—a rounded horn above its nostrils and a horn in front of each eye. It also had small, bony scales on its body.

COUNT
how many of each theropod you can see. Answers on pp. 92–93.

Ceratosaurus

Who's who?

Sauropods were the largest land animals to have lived on Earth. They were plant-eating dinosaurs that used their incredibly long necks to reach high treetops. Their enormous appetite was a perfect match for their huge size.

1

2

MATCH
the descriptions to the dinosaurs. See answers on pp. 92–93.

Apatosaurus

Apatosaurus's neck was long and flexible. It had a **long tail**, which it may have cracked like a **whip**. Its head was small in comparison to its huge body.

Saltasaurus

Saltasaurus was one of the smallest sauropods. It had **bony plates** on its back that acted as **body armor**. Saltasaurus had strong legs like an elephant, and no toes on its front feet.

Brachiosaurus

Brachiosaurus had a long neck like a giraffe. With its spoon-like teeth, it fed on leaves of tree ferns and conifers. It also had a **large crest** above its eyes.

Diplodocus

With a tail as long as the rest of its body, Diplodocus was one of the longest ever land animals. It had **spiky, triangular plates** along its back, neck, and tail.

Thyreophorans

Thyreophorans were plant-eating dinosaurs that walked on all fours. They had rows of armored plates that ran along their necks, backs, and tails.

CONNECT the dots to reveal the picture and then color it in.

Edmontonia

Edmontonia used the enormous spikes on its shoulders to defend itself against predators.

Huayangosaurus

Like Stegosaurus, Huayangosaurus had huge back plates and tail spikes. However, Huayangosaurus's plates were more pointy. It also had spikes on its shoulders.

Facts about...

Armor

Some thyreophorans, such as Euoplocephalus, had **armored plates** on their eyelids! Liaoningosaurus had one over its belly, while Polacanthus had a protective shield over its hips.

Ankylosaurus

With its armored body and huge clubbed tail, the herbivorous Ankylosaurus was a tough opponent to defeat.

Stegosaurus

Stegosaurus had two rows of big, bony plates. Although it was around the size of an elephant, Stegosaurus's brain was no bigger than an apple!

25

Find the
winner

Ornithopods were plant-eaters. Many had beaks for gathering leaves. Some ornithopods could walk on both two or four legs.

Facts about...

Tenontosaurus

Tenontosaurus used its **U-shaped beak** to chomp on plants. It was 26 ft (8 m) long. Fossils suggest that it may have been hunted by packs of Deinonychus who were relatively smaller than Tenontosaurus.

FOLLOW the lines to find out which dinosaur gets to eat.

Facts about...

Hypsilophodon

Hypsilophodon used its **powerful legs** to run swiftly. It had big eyes that gave it excellent vision.

Facts about...

Parasaurolophus

Parasaurolophus was 30 ft (9 m) long. It traveled in herds. The **hollow crest** on Parasaurolophus's head helped it to make loud noises.

Hard-headed

Marginocephalians were herbivores that lived mainly in the Cretaceous period. They used their thick, bony skulls for defense. Pachycephalosaurus belonged to this group.

GUESS if the statements are true or false. Answers on pp. 92–93.

The bony dome on its head was 10 in (25 cm) thick.

These spikes may have been used for show or defense.

Three of its toes were spread out to help this dinosaur carry its weight as it walked on two legs. The fourth toe was held aloft.

True or False?

1. Pachycephalosaurus was a herbivore.

2. The skull of Pachycephalosaurus was 18 in (45 cm) thick.

3. Pachycephalosaurus may have used its head like a battering ram.

4. Marginocephalians lived in the Triassic period.

Pachycephalosaurus's skin may have had a bumpy surface.

This dinosaur ran swiftly with its long, sturdy legs.

Facts about...

The skull

It is believed that during a fight, Pachycephalosaurus may have used its **bony head** like a battering ram. They probably also banged their heads together to show off how powerful they were.

29

Age of the dinosaurs

Dinosaurs, such as Tyrannosaurus and Triceratops, along with other prehistoric creatures became extinct 66 million years ago, but they still fascinate us to this day.

FIND

where these pictures
are on pp. 32–45.
Check your answers
on pp. 92–93.

7

8

9

10

11

12

Flying high with
pterosaurs

While dinosaurs ruled the land, pterosaurs owned the sky. These flying reptiles had hollow bones and small bodies, but could have wingspans of up to 36 ft (11 m).

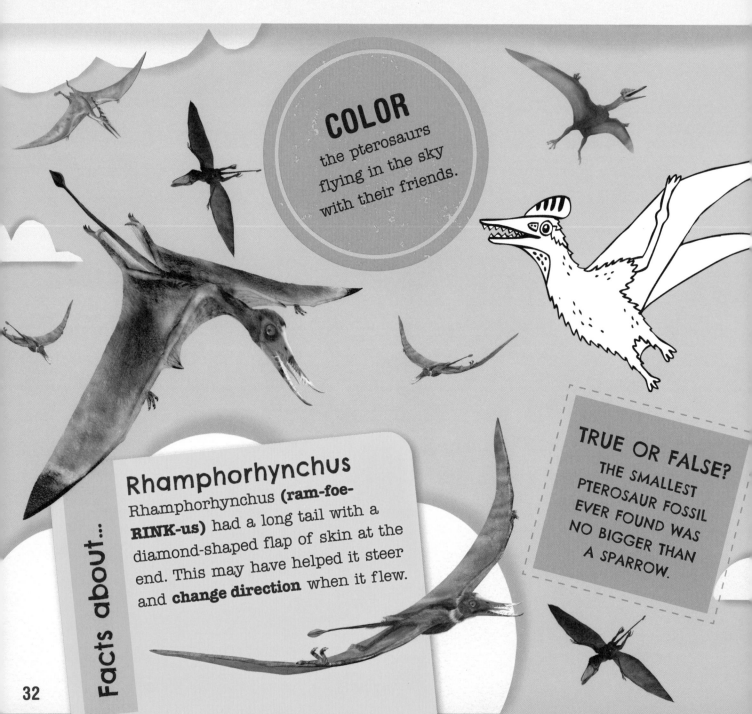

COLOR
the pterosaurs flying in the sky with their friends.

Rhamphorhynchus
Rhamphorhynchus (**ram-foe-RINK-us**) had a long tail with a diamond-shaped flap of skin at the end. This may have helped it steer and **change direction** when it flew.

Facts about...

TRUE OR FALSE?
THE SMALLEST PTEROSAUR FOSSIL EVER FOUND WAS NO BIGGER THAN A SPARROW.

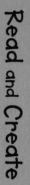

Facts about...

Dimorphodon

Its **unusually large head** was around a third of its body length, and contained two types of teeth—perfect for trapping prey.

Facts about...

Pteranodon

This pterosaur was given its name (pteranodon means **"wing without tooth"**) after fossil collectors discovered it had **no teeth** at all.

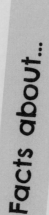

Facts about...

Pterodactylus

One of the best known pterosaurs, it had a short tail and long neck, and its wings were covered in a leathery material that helped it to **fly quickly**.

The mixed-up scrap-book

Oops! Someone has mixed up the labels in their dinosaur scrapbook. Can you use the clues on the tags to figure out which is which?

Mamenchisaurus

- Walked on four legs.
- Was an herbivore.
- Had one of the longest necks of any animal in history.
- Had strong, thick skin.

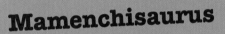

Dimorphodon

- Had a large head and beak.
- Its tail was fairly thin.
- Was actually a pterosaur, not a dinosaur.
- Its wings were made of skin.

Baryonyx

- Had a narrow hump along its back.
- Its head looked a little like a crocodile's.
- Walked on its hind legs.
- Had a long, slender skull.

Are you a dino EXPERT?

3

Pentaceratops

- Was a herbivore.
- Walked on four legs.
- Had a large beak.
- Used its horns for defense.
- Had a large, armored skull.

MATCH

the descriptions to the dinosaurs. See answers on pp. 92–93.

4

5

Giganotosaurus

- Had short forearms with sharp claws.
- Was a relative of Tyrannosaurus.
- Walked on strong hind legs.
- Had razor-sharp teeth.

MATCH the marine reptiles with their descriptions. Check your answers on pp. 92–93.

TRUE OR FALSE?
MARINE REPTILES ARE DINOSAURS THAT SWIM.

Under the sea

Dinosaurs were land-based creatures, but during the time they walked on the Earth, another group of creatures called marine reptiles lurked underwater.

Facts about...

Pliosaurus

This giant beast (seen below) grew to up to 40 ft (12 m) long and was one of the **deadliest marine reptiles** of all time.

4

c

Ichthyosaurus

- Had a small, slim snout.
- Its body was shaped like a dolphin's.
- Had large eyes compared to its size.

a

Metriorhynchus

- It looked a little like a prehistoric crocodile.
- Had a long, powerful tail with a large fin at the back.

b

Elasmosaurus

- Its neck was as long as its entire body.
- Its head was very small compared to its body.
- Had four large flippers.

d

Lariosaurus

- It had paddles instead of front legs, with claws at the back.
- Its tail was thin, with no fin at the back.

Dinosaur puzzles

Dinosaurs came in all shapes and sizes. How well do you think you can tell them apart? Find out with these puzzles.

1

GUESS the dinosaur using the clues on these pages. Answers on pp. 92–93.

2

3

Einiosaurus

This dinosaur had a **long, curved horn** on its head. It also had two spiky horns sticking out from its neck frill. Einiosaurus grew up to 20 ft (6 m) long.

Euoplocephalus

Euoplocephalus used its **heavy club tail** to defend itself from predators. Completely covered in armored plates, this dinosaur's only weak spot was its soft belly.

4

Spinosaurus

This massive predator from the late Cretaceous period was famous for the large **sail-like spine** on its back. It feasted on fish, birds, turtles, and other dinosaurs.

Saltasaurus

Saltasaurus had a **long neck**, though it was shorter than the necks of most other sauropods. This herbivore from the late Cretaceous period was one of the last dinosaurs to exist.

A- maze -ing escape!

Life wasn't always easy for a dinosaur. Some of them, such as Tenontosaurus, couldn't easily defend themselves from attackers, and hungry predators could be lurking around every corner!

START

DRAW

a safe route through the maze. Check the box by each predator you spot.

How do you say the names of these dinosaurs?

Hungry predators

Utahraptor

YOU-tah-RAP-tor
Most famous for its deadly claws, it was a fierce hunter.

Giganotosaurus

gig-AN-oh-toe-SORE-rus
This was a distant relative of Tyrannosaurus that lived around thirty million years earlier.

Tyrannosaurus

TIE-ran-oh-SORE-us
This was the king of dinosaurs, and maybe the most fearsome predator of all.

Carnotaurus

CAR-no-TAWR-us
Carnotaurus was a fairly large predator with thick horns above its eyes.

Deinonychus

dye-NON-ee-cuss
This was a small, but deadly pack hunter from the Cretaceous period.

Spinosaurus

SPINE-oh-SORE-us
The largest predator to ever walk the Earth.

I only eat plants, but these dinosaurs are scary!

Tenontosaurus

ten-NON-toe-SORE-us

END

Great job! But now I'm hungry...

41

How many dinosaurs?

Do you have a good eye? There are three species of dinosaurs on these pages. How many of each type can you spot? Check your answers on pp. 92–93.

COUNT the total number of Tyrannosaurus you can spot.

Tyrannosaurus

Check your answers on pp. 92–93.

Facts about...

Tyrannosaurus

Full name Tyrannosaurus rex, it stood 13 ft (4 m) tall at the hips and 40 ft (13 m) long, making it one of the most **ferocious beasts** to ever live.

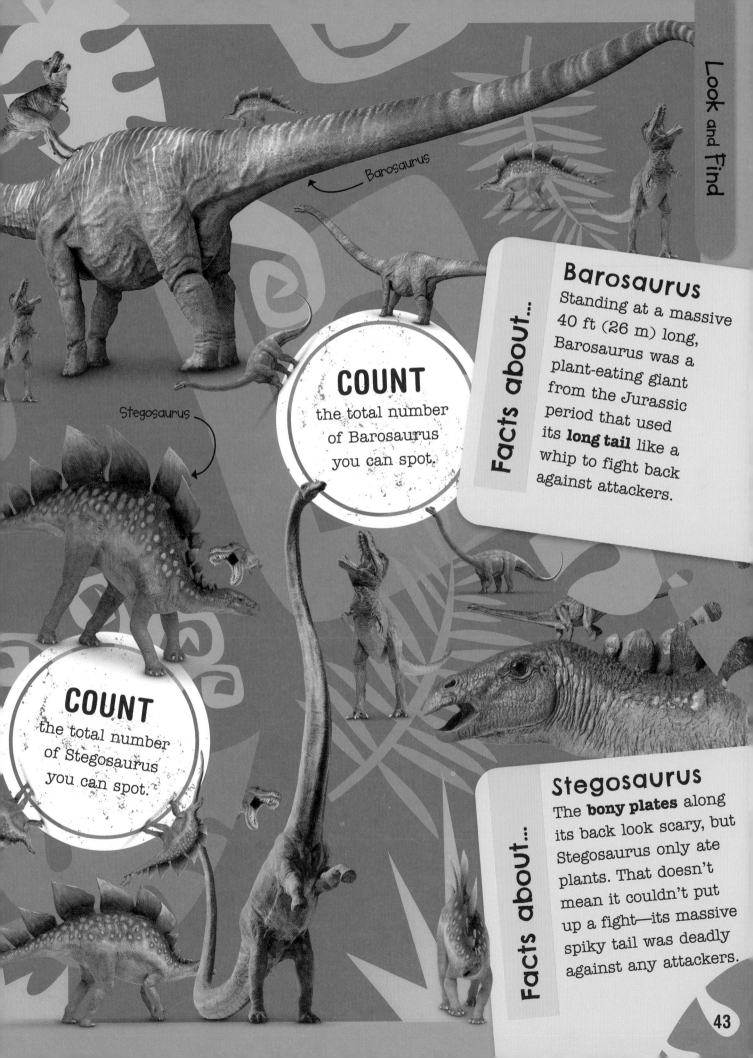

→ Barosaurus

Stegosaurus →

COUNT the total number of Barosaurus you can spot.

Facts about...

Barosaurus

Standing at a massive 40 ft (26 m) long, Barosaurus was a plant-eating giant from the Jurassic period that used its **long tail** like a whip to fight back against attackers.

COUNT the total number of Stegosaurus you can spot.

Facts about...

Stegosaurus

The **bony plates** along its back look scary, but Stegosaurus only ate plants. That doesn't mean it couldn't put up a fight—its massive spiky tail was deadly against any attackers.

43

Picture gallery

Theropods

These meat-eaters were the deadliest hunters of the dinosaur age.

Pterodactylus

One of the famous pterosaurs, it had a short neck and long tail that helped it fly.

Archaeopteryx

Archaeopteryx was one of the first bird-like dinosaurs.

Brachiosaurus

This sauropod used its long neck to reach high treetops.

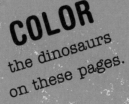

COLOR the dinosaurs on these pages.

Deinosuchus

Deinosuchus was a relative of the alligators. It had fearsome jaws and a powerful bite.

Cryolophosaurus

....

....

....

COLOR the scene and write a description in the box.

Dinosaur life

Even though the world was a very different place when dinosaurs ruled the Earth, dinosaurs had a lot more in common with modern animals than you might think.

FIND where these pictures are on pp. 48–71. Check your answers on pp. 92–93.

7

8

9

10

11

12

Baby dinosaurs

In the same way as birds do, mother dinosaurs, such as Maiasaura, laid eggs in nests. After hatching from their eggs, baby dinosaurs were either cared for by their parents or had to support themselves.

GUESS the answers to questions in the quiz box. Answers on pp. 92–93.

Baby Maiasaura had flat skulls and big eyes.

They may have had a scaly, patterned skin.

The babies were 12 in (30 cm) long at birth.

Facts about...

Maiasaura

Maiasaura means "**good mother lizard**." It lived in herds that may have raised their babies together. Maiasaura was also the first dinosaur in space! Small pieces of its bone and shell were blasted off into space on board a rocket in 1985.

The mother Maiasaura was 30 ft (9 m) long—almost as long as a bus.

Young Maiasaura stayed around their mothers while growing up.

Quiz

1 What does the name "Maiasaura" mean?

a. Good mother lizard
b. Big lizard
c. Yellow dinosaur
d. Mother lizard

2 How long was a mother Maisasura?

a. 6.5 ft (2 m)
b. 13 ft (4 m)
c. 30 ft (9 m)
d. 36 ft (11 m)

3 In which year were small pieces of Maiasaura bones and shells carried to space?

a. 1977
b. 1979
c. 1985
d. 1987

4 How long are Maiasaura babies at birth?

a. 10 in (25 cm)
b. 12 in (30 cm)
c. 14 in (35 cm)
d. 17 in (45 cm)

Save the eggs

A Maiasaura has been separated from her babies. Find something to use as counters and help guide her back to her nest.

Start

Roll a die and move th[e] correct numb[er] of steps alo[ng] the board.

10
Egg fact
Some species of dinosaurs would sit on their nests in a similar way chickens sit on their eggs today.

9
A Brachiosaurus offers you a shortcut. **GO FORWARD** to step 22.

8

11

12
You're being chased! Climb a vine to escape and **GO BACK** to step 1.

13

14
You get slowed down by a passing herd. **MISS A TURN**.

15

Finish

24
An Ankylosaur[us] is blocking yo[ur] path. **ROLL A SIX TO END THE GAME.**

50

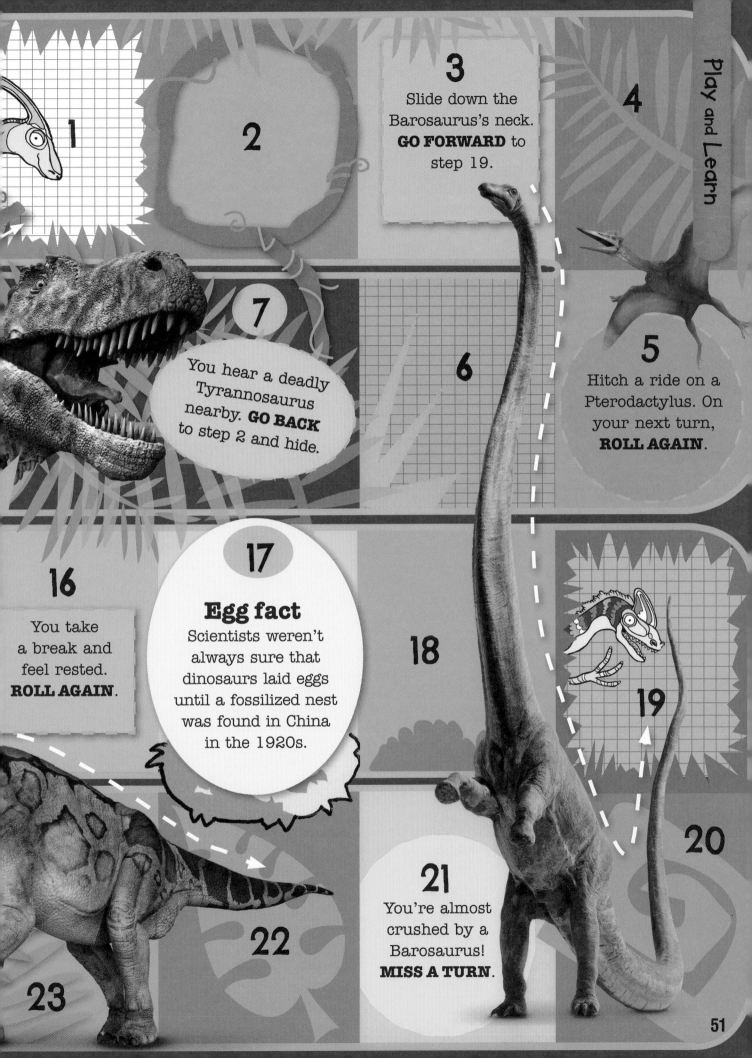

1

2

3
Slide down the Barosaurus's neck. **GO FORWARD** to step 19.

4

5
Hitch a ride on a Pterodactylus. On your next turn, **ROLL AGAIN**.

7
You hear a deadly Tyrannosaurus nearby. **GO BACK** to step 2 and hide.

6

16
You take a break and feel rested. **ROLL AGAIN**.

17
Egg fact
Scientists weren't always sure that dinosaurs laid eggs until a fossilized nest was found in China in the 1920s.

18

19

20

23

22

21
You're almost crushed by a Barosaurus! **MISS A TURN**.

Who gets dinner?

Only some dinosaurs, like Iguanodon, could defend themselves against attackers. If they couldn't run away they would probably end up being another dinosaur's, such as Utahraptor's, dinner!

FIND which path leads to the dinosaur in the middle.

Facts about... Utahraptor

One of the deadliest dinosaurs of the early Cretaceous period, Utahraptor had a huge **hooked claw** on each foot that it would use to attack its prey.

Facts about... Iguanodon

The plant-eating Iguanodon was around the same size as an elephant. It used its sharp **thumb-like spike** to defend itself from other dinosaurs.

END

Copy the SCENE

Are you a budding artist? By copying each square in this grid you'll be able to draw a great dinosaur scene in no time.

Spot the dinosaurs in the image.

Stegosaurus

Triceratops

Pterodactylus

Tyrannosaurus

1 - - - - - - - - - - - - - - - -

2 - - - - - - - - - - - - - - - -

3 - - - - - - - - - - - - - - - -

4 - - - - - - - - - - - - - - - -

Check your answers on pp. 92–93.

Home sweet home

Dinosaurs lived in several different places (habitats). There were six main habitats, and where they lived depended on the climate or how much food there was.

Mountains

There probably wasn't much food here, but dinosaur fossils have been found near mountains.

b

Forests

a

The trees in forests were a rich source of food for many plant-eaters.

Swampland

c

Swamps were perfect for both fish-eating and plant-eating dinosaurs.

1 *I liked to be in wet areas with trees and fish.*

2 *There weren't that many plants where I lived.*

3 *I lived in a very hot, dry, and dusty place.*

Spinosaurus

Plateosaurus

Gallimimus

MATCH

the dinosaurs to the habitats based on the clues. Answers on pp. 92–93.

Desert plains **e**

The Earth was hotter than it is today, with vast deserts all over. Some dinosaurs adapted to live in these dry places.

Riverbanks **d**

All living things need water to survive, so a lot of dinosaurs lived by rivers and coasts.

Scrubland **f**

Not too many plants grew here, but scrubland was home to many early dinosaurs.

I sometimes lived high up, by a lot of rocks.

The place I lived had plenty of water.

There were a lot of tasty trees where I lived.

4 Edmontonia

5 Herrerasaurus

6 Stegosaurus

Dinosaur diets

Some dinosaurs were carnivores, which means they ate meat. Others were herbivores, which means they ate plants. Finally, there were some dinosaurs that ate both plants and meat—these were omnivores.

Oviraptor

Oviraptor may have been an omnivore. It is thought to have chowed down on insects, lizards, and plants.

Gallimimus

With its sturdy legs and light weight, Gallimimus ran fast—it was one of the speediest dinosaurs ever. This dinosaur swallowed stones that helped with digestion. Gallimimus would eat leaves and the stones would grind the leaves up in its belly.

Therizinosaurus

Unlike most other meat-eating theropods, Therizinosaurus ate plants. It had three large, almost sword-like claws that were probably used for defense.

GUESS the answers to the questions. Check your answers on pp. 92–93.

Heterodontosaurus

This turkey-sized dinosaur had several types of teeth, including long fangs. The fangs may have been used for fighting, rather than eating, though.

Quiz

1 What did Oviraptor eat?

2 Why did Gallimimus swallow stones?

3 What did Heterodontosaurus use its fangs for?

4 What did Therizinosaurus eat?

Hunter and
hunted

For carnivores, dinner was often another dinosaur! Sometimes smaller dinosaurs made a meal of one much bigger than themselves.

Start

Deinonychus

This ferocious hunter from the early Cretaceous period is named "terrible claw" because of the deadly claws on its feet.

CONNECT

the dots to reveal the rest of the picture, then color it in.

Facts about...

Hunting

When taking on a bigger dinosaur, a group of smaller predators may have **ganged up** to attack it together. Many modern animals, such as hyenas and wolves, do this, too.

Dinosaur defense

Some dinosaurs could attack predators to avoid being eaten. Others, like Ankylosaurus, had special defensive features, such as plates and spines.

Dryosaurus

- This herbivore's sturdy legs helped it quickly run away from danger.
- It may have used its stiff tail to take sharp turns and avoid obstacles while escaping an attack.
- Dryosaurus had short, weak arms.

1 What did Dryosaurus use its tail for?

Styracosaurus

- Unlike most dinosaurs, Styracosaurus had horns, frills, and spikes. However, its frill spikes were only for display.
- It probably used its nose horn, which was 20 in (50 cm) long, to fight.
- Small spikes may have ran along this dinosaur's back and tail.

2 How long was Styracosaurus's nose horn?

Ankylosaurus

- Ankylosaurus was covered in hundreds of bony plates.
- With a huge club tail as its main weapon, this dinosaur was a master of defense.
- Ankylosaurus had tough bony plates—called osteoderms—on its neck, back, and tail.

3 What was Ankylosaurus's main weapon?

GUESS

the answers to the questions. Check your answers on pp. 92–93.

Sauropelta

- Sauropelta's neck spines were probably used for both defense and display.
- This plant-eater had studded armor on its back, similar to a knight's chain mail.
- Sauropelta may have been hunted by packs of Deinonychus, small meat-eaters.

4 Which small dinosaur used to attack Sauropelta?

Plant-eaters

Most dinosaurs were plant-eaters. These dinosaurs were different shapes and sizes. They ate ferns and leaves for a large part of their day.

1

c

Barosaurus

Like all sauropods, Barosaurus had a small head, long neck, and a bulky body. It may have also had spines running along its back.

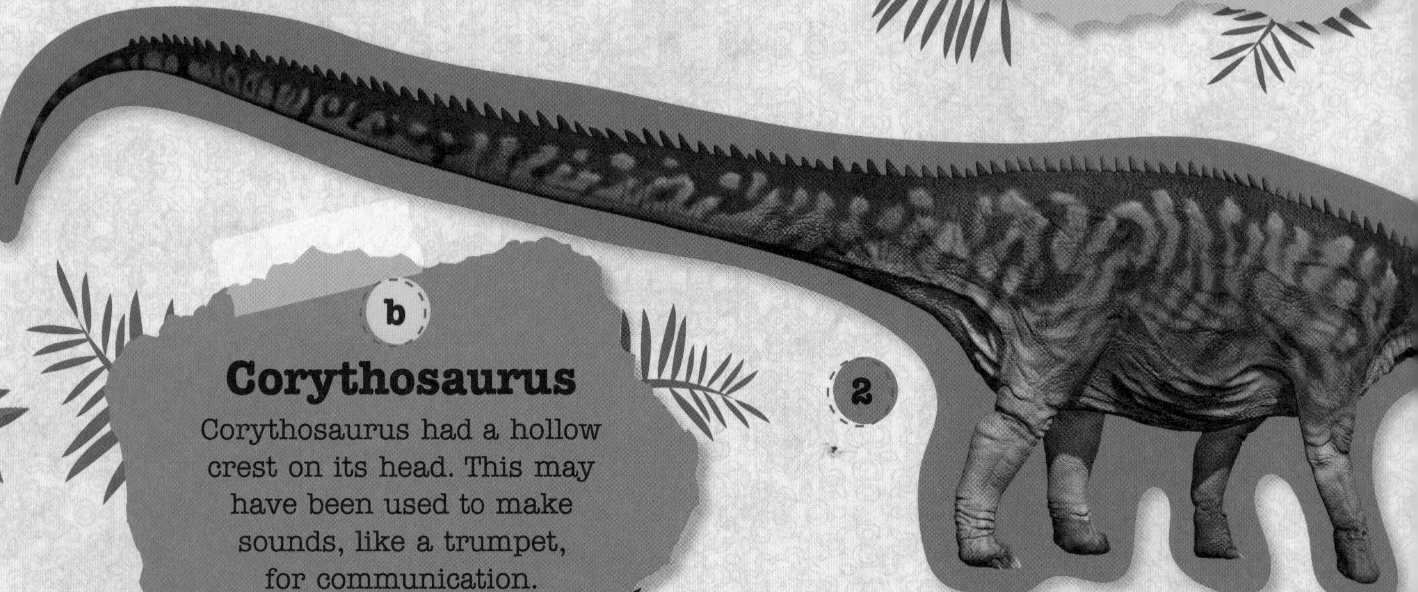

b

Corythosaurus

Corythosaurus had a hollow crest on its head. This may have been used to make sounds, like a trumpet, for communication.

2

3

d

Euoplocephalus

Euoplocephalus swung its heavy club tail at huge predators, such as Albertosaurus. The spikes on its back were meant for extra protection.

MATCH
the descriptions to each dinosaur. See answers on pp. 92–93.

a

Australotitan cooperensis

Measuring 80–98 ft (25–30 m) long, Australotitan cooperensis was as long as a basketball court. It is believed to be one of the largest dinosaurs ever.

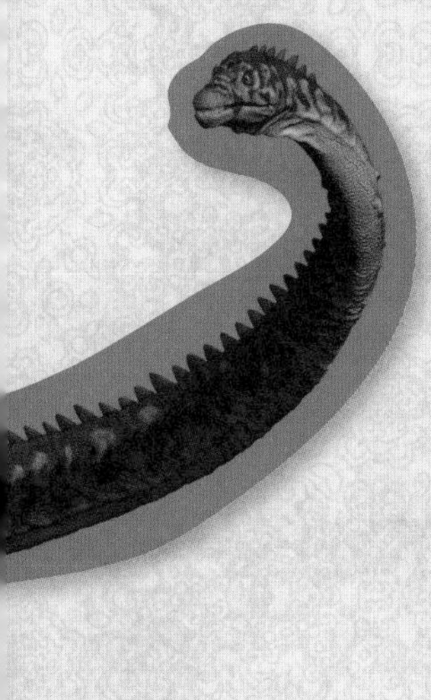

4

Tyrannosaurus
trouble

Meat-eating dinosaurs had sharp teeth and long claws. Tyrannosaurus was the most fearsome predator in the Cretaceous period. It could crush prey in just a single bite!

CONNECT the dots to reveal the rest of the picture, then color it in.

OTHER MEAT-EATERS

Staurikosaurus

Staurikosaurus was a little bigger than an average toddler. It was agile and could run swiftly because it was lightly built.

Start

Facts about...

Diet

Most paleontologists agree that, like most predators, if a meal was easily available, such as an already **dead animal**, Tyrannosaurus would have eaten it. However, if a free meal was not available, it would have chased down and **hunted prey**.

Baryonyx

Baryonyx's long, narrow jaws and pointy teeth were perfectly suited for feeding on fish and dinosaurs.

Albertosaurus

Albertosaurus may have used its powerful jaws to prey on herbivores as large as itself.

What color were they?

Since fossils (remains of prehistoric life) are made of stone, it's tricky to identify what color most dinosaurs were. But experts do know the colors of some of them!

COLOR in the dinosaurs. Read the facts to help you decide how to make them look.

Facts about...

Blending in

Some animals blend into the environment while hunting prey. A tiger's stripes keep it **hidden in tall grass**. Some dinosaurs may have been able to blend in, too.

Facts about...

Standing out

Peacocks and many other animals are colorful so they can **attract a mate** or threaten enemies. Some dinosaurs also had ways of standing out.

Facts about...

Being plain

Animals such as elephants don't have many predators, so don't need to blend in or stand out. It's likely **many dinosaurs were plain**, too.

69

spot the difference

the difference These two pictures may look the same, but are slightly different! Look carefully and try to find the five differences.

TRUE OR FALSE?
THE WORD "DINOSAUR" MEANS "FRIGHTENING REPTILE."

Facts about...

Spinosaurus

At 52 ft (16 m) long, Spinosaurus was one of the **biggest predators** to have existed. Its diet was mainly made up of giant fish. This dinosaur may even have been able to "sense" fish with the help of the holes on its snout, like a crocodile.

SPOT the **five** differences between the two pictures.

Studying dinosaurs

Experts called paleontologists dedicate their lives to studying fossils (the remains of prehistoric creatures) so that we can all learn more about these amazing animals.

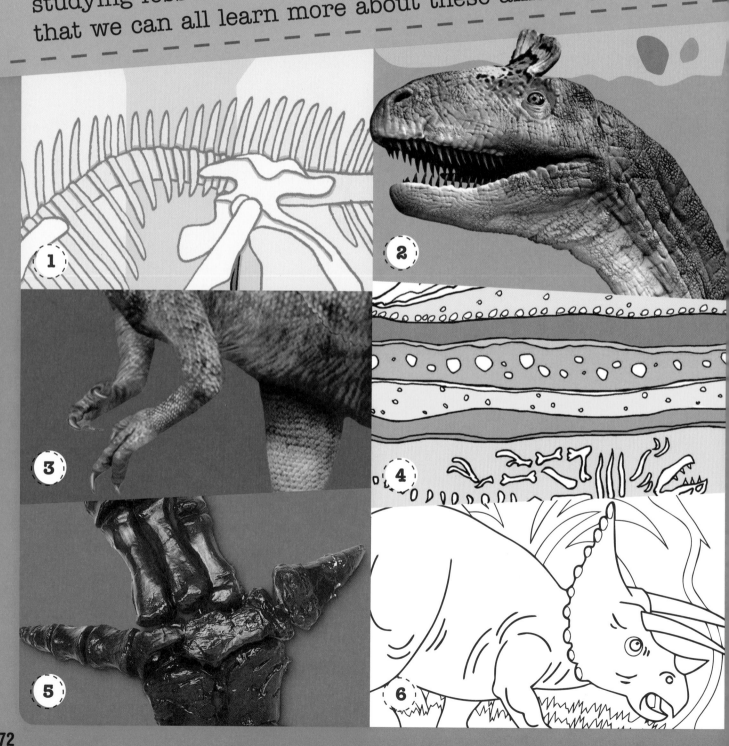

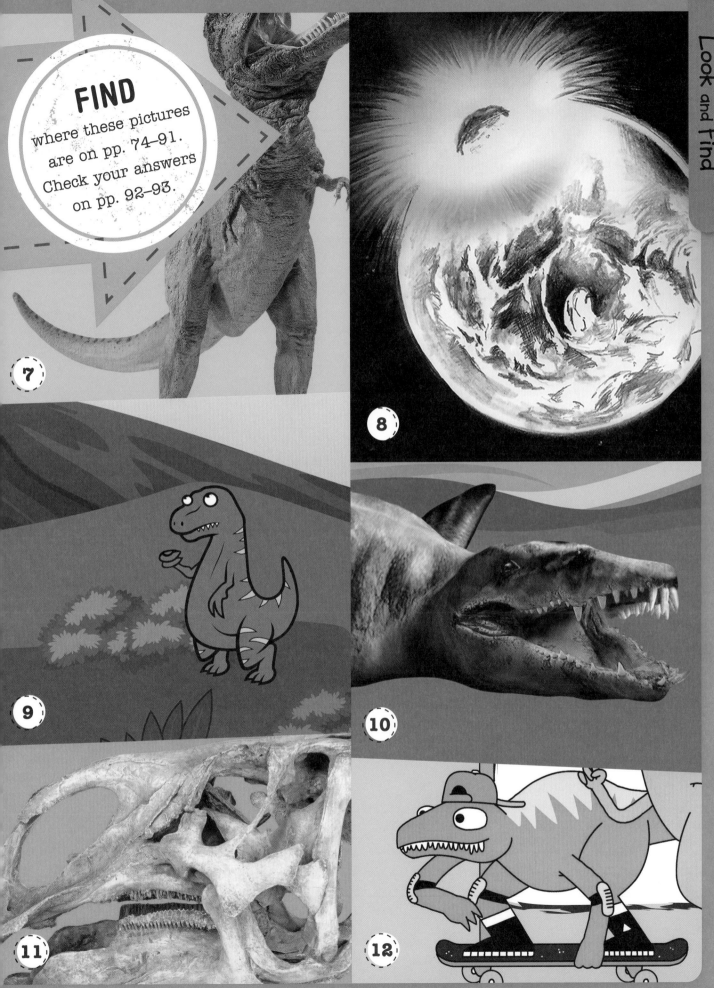

FIND
where these pictures are on pp. 74–91. Check your answers on pp. 92–93.

7

8

9

10

11

12

The great extinction

Dinosaurs ruled the Earth for millions of years. But 66 million years ago, a giant asteroid struck the Earth causing almost all of them to die out and become extinct.

Scientists think the asteroid was about 6 miles (10 km) wide.

How it happened

The asteroid struck the Earth with such force that it caused earthquakes, tsunamis, and threw a cloud of dust into the sky, blocking out the sun.

"Extinct" means "no longer existing."

Are they all gone?

While dinosaurs as we think of them are all gone, modern birds are the last remaining group—making birds the only **surviving dinosaurs**!

Small mammals like this Nemegtbaatar survived.

Facts about...

Survivors

No land animals bigger than a dog survived the **mass extinction**, but other animals, such as fish, lizards, insects, and small mammals, did.

Quiz

1 How many years ago did the asteroid hit the Earth?

a. 60 million years ago
b. 66 million years ago
c. 90 million years ago

2 How big was the asteroid that struck the Earth?

a. 4.6 miles (7.5 km)
b. 6 miles (10 km)
c. 9.3 miles (15 km)

3 What are the only surviving dinosaurs?

a. Birds
b. Sauropods
c. Marine reptiles

4 What does "extinct" mean?

a. Living even now
b. No longer existing
c. Badly injured

GUESS
the anwers to the questions. Check your answers on pp. 92–93.

Tupandactylus

What happened to the pterosaurs?

Pterosaurs were flying reptiles that appeared in the Triassic period. They survived for 150 million years before facing mass extinction in the Cretaceous period.

Did all the marine reptiles die?

Like the pterosaurs and dinosaurs, many marine reptiles did not survive the asteroid crash.

Mosasaurus

Extinction scene

The mass extinction wiped out seventy-five percent of life on Earth. In addition to the asteroid collision, volcanic eruptions released poisonous gases into the air. This led to the end of the age of the dinosaurs.

SPOT everything listed in the box.

Around sixty percent of the plants on Earth were also destroyed forever.

What can you spot?

1 Mountains

2 Clouds

3 Asteroid

4 Pond

5 Shrubs

6 Triceratops

7 Sauropod

8 Pentaceratops

77

How fossils are made...

It takes a very long time for fossils to form, and some of the earliest discovered are almost 3.5 billion years old!

COLOR in the rest of the comic to finish off the story of fossilization.

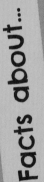

Facts about...

Fossilization

Living things can only become fossils if they are **buried quickly** after death. Otherwise they simply decay, or rot, and disappear. This is why fossils are so rare.

TRUE OR FALSE?
SEA CREATURES CAN'T TURN INTO FOSSILS.

70 million years ago...

1 A dinosaur has died and its body quickly sinks into thick mud, burying it and protecting it from the elements.

2 million years ago...

4 The Earth's plates have shifted even more and a mountain range has formed above the fossil.

Five years later...

2 Its flesh has slowly rotted away leaving just the bones—which have split apart and are buried under the ground.

50 million years ago...

3 The Earth's plates have shifted and a sea has spread over the area. Pressure has made the mud and sand harden.

Present day...

What's that over there in the sand?

It looks like a bone, but it's so big!

5 Over a long period of time, layers on top of the fossil have been worn away by extreme weather. Then one day a bone is spotted and paleontologists can dig up the pieces of the fossil.

Dinosaurs and their fossils

Fossils are the physical remains and traces of animals and plants that have been dead for thousands to millions of years. Scientists study fossils to know how much life has changed on Earth over a period of time.

1

2

A

Tyrannosaurus

B

Deinonychus

Stone clues

Without fossils we would know very little about dinosaurs and prehistoric life. By **studying fossils**, scientists can find clues about a dinosaur's size, shape, diet, and more.

Facts about...

Fossil experts are called paleontologists.

MATCH

the creatures to their fossils. Check your answers on pp. 92–93.

3

5

4

E Pterodactylus

C Triceratops

D Diplodocus

Facts about...

Excavation

It can be a very long and difficult job to get fossils out of the ground because they can be stuck between **layers of hard rock** that have to be broken up bit by bit.

81

Draw your own
dinosaur

Drawing a dinosaur might seem hard, but it's not if you break it into steps. Get started by drawing this little Compsognathus.

Step 1

Start by lightly copying this frame in pencil to determine how big your dinosaur will be. Add circles for the head, body, and limbs as shown.

Step 2

Draw the outline of your dinosaur, using the circles as a guide. Don't worry about adding detail yet—just focus on the basic shape.

Step 3

Use an eraser to get rid of the guides. Add details such as claws, eyes, and teeth. Finally, color it in!

I'm about the same size as a Compsognathus!

DRAW a Compsognathus in the space below. Don't forget to practice!

Facts about...

Compsognathus

One of the smallest predatory dinosaurs ever was **Compsognathus (COMP-sog-NAITH-us)**, which was only around the size of a big chicken! Amazingly, despite its size, it may have been able to reach speeds of up to 25 mph (40 kph)!

Dino dig
notes

With so many species of dinosaurs, pterosaurs, and marine reptiles, experts take notes to help them keep track. Match the pictures to help finish off the research.

1

2

3

4

5

6

MATCH the pictures of the creatures with their silhouettes. Answers on pp. 92–93.

a Ouranosaurus
(ooh-RAN-uh-SAWR-us)

- **LENGTH:** Up to 23 ft (7 m)
- **FOUND IN:** Desert plains
- **FOOD:** Plants
- **LIVED:** Early Cretaceous

b Efraasia
(E-FRAHS-ee-A)

- **LENGTH:** Up to 23 ft (7 m)
- **FOUND IN:** Forests
- **FOOD:** Plants
- **LIVED:** Late Triassic

c Piatnitzkysaurus
(PEA-at-NITS-key-SORE-us)

- **LENGTH:** Up to 16 ft (5 m)
- **FOUND IN:** Forests
- **FOOD:** Meat
- **LIVED:** Early Jurassic

d Ichthyosaurus
(ICK-thee-oh-SORE-uss)

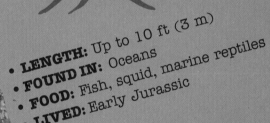

- **LENGTH:** Up to 10 ft (3 m)
- **FOUND IN:** Oceans
- **FOOD:** Fish, squid, marine reptiles
- **LIVED:** Early Jurassic

e Mosasaurus
(MOSE-ah-saw-rus)

- **LENGTH:** Up to 50 ft (15 m)
- **FOUND IN:** Oceans
- **FOOD:** Marine reptiles, fish, squid
- **LIVED:** Late Cretaceous

f Cryolophosaurus
(CRY-oh-loaf-oh-SAWR-us)

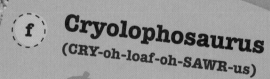

- **LENGTH:** Up to 26 ft (8 m)
- **FOUND IN:** Forests
- **FOOD:** Meat
- **LIVED:** Early Jurassic

Inside the
museum

Museums all over the world have amazing fossil collections you can go and visit. Seeing dinosaur skeletons up close gives you a much better idea of how big they were.

Facts about...

Hadrosaurids

Parasaurolophus belonged to a group of dinosaurs called hadrosaurids. This group of plant-eating dinosaurs from the late Cretaceous period were famous for their **strange-shaped heads**.

Parasaurolophus

Parasaurolophus **(PA-ra-SORE-oh-LOAF-US)**, is famous for its **long, curved skull crest**, which it might have used like a trumpet to warn its herd of danger.

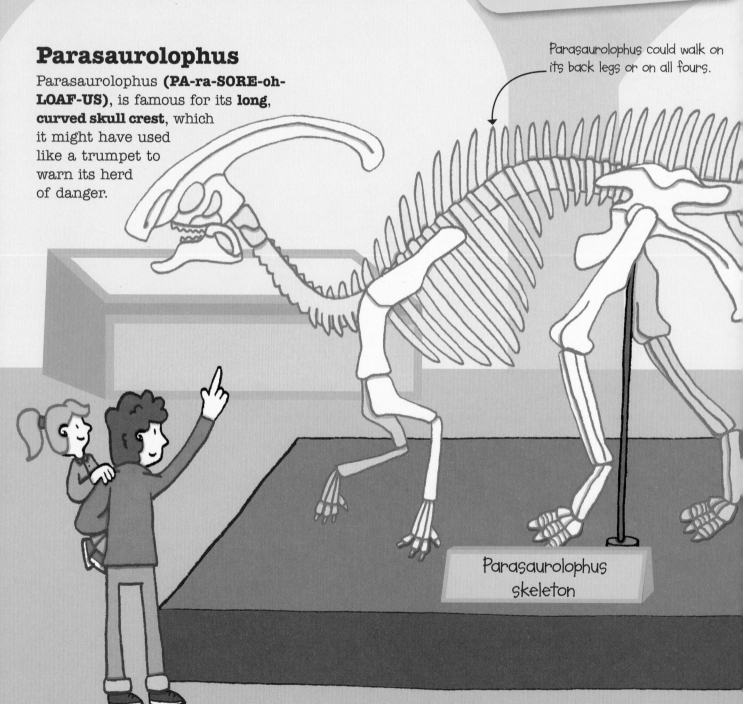

Parasaurolophus could walk on its back legs or on all fours.

Parasaurolophus skeleton

Hadrosaur skulls

1 **Corythosaurus** had a small snout with a rounded crest at the top of its head.

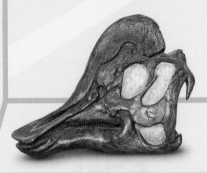

2 **Lambeosaurus** had a narrow mouth and a crest that resembled an axe blade.

3 **Brachylophosaurus** had a deep snout and a rectangle-shaped skull that was flat on top.

All hadrosaurids had strong, stiff tails.

COLOR in the Parasaurolophus model.

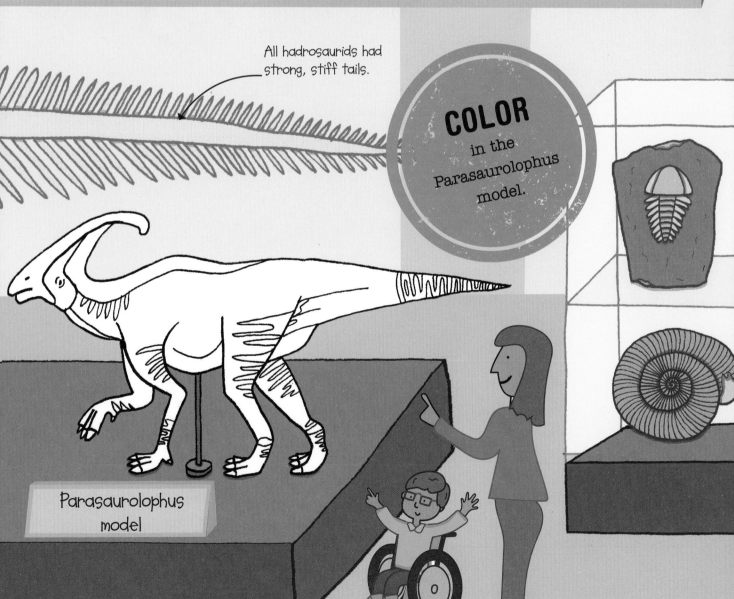

Parasaurolophus model

Match the fossils

Fossils can be found almost anywhere! Once discovered, they are dug up and studied by paleontologists. Here are some amazing finds.

FOLLOW the lines to match the animal with its fossil.

Megalodon

Hand

Arm

Archaeopteryx

Deinocheirus

Iguanodon

TRUE OR FALSE?
ALL FOSSILS
WERE ONCE
LIVING THINGS.

Tooth

Body

My favorite creatures

COLOR
in the creatures in
each frame.

Ankylosaurus
This slow-moving dinosaur
ate low-lying plants.

Tyrannosaurus
Only the fastest dinosaurs
could escape the mighty
Tyrannosaurus.

Triceratops
Triceratops had a
parrot-like beak and
teeth like scissors.

Quetzalcoatlus
This pterosaur may
have been the biggest
flying animal on Earth.

Mosasaurus
Mosasaurus had flexible
jaws and a flat, long tail.

Mamenchisaurus
Mamenchisaurus
weighed around
55 tons (50 tonnes).

Answers

8–9
1. Diamond-shaped
2. Three
3. A chicken
4. Using its long neck

10–11
True or False?
True

12–13
True or False?
False

Plateosaurus: 2
Herrerasaurus: 3
Thecodontosaurus: 6
Pisanosaurus: 2
Eoraptor: 3

16–17
1. Triassic period
2. Around 80 million years
3. Africa

20–21
Coelophysis: 10
Allosaurus: 11
Ceratosaurus: 8

22–23
1. Brachiosaurus
2. Diplodocus
3. Saltasaurus
4. Apatosaurus

28–29
1. True
2. False
3. True
4. False

11. Page 45
12. Page 37

32–33
True or False?
True

34–35
1. Giganotosaurus
2. Pentaceratops
3. Dimorphodon
4. Baryonyx
5. Mamenchisaurus

36–37
True or False?
False

1c, 2a, 3b, 4d

38–39
1. Einiosaurus
2. Saltasaurus
3. Euoplocephalus
4. Spinosaurus

42–43
Tyrannosaurus: 22
Barosaurus: 10
Stegosaurus: 12

46–47
1. Page 59
2. Page 51
3. Page 57

4. Page 61
5. Pages 48–49
6. Page 68
7. Page 54
8. Page 56
9. Page 57
10. Page 70
11. Page 50
12. Page 62

48–49
1a, 2c, 3c, 4b

54–55
1. Pterodactylus
2. Stegosaurus
3. Tyrannosaurus
4. Triceratops

56–57
1c, 2f, 3e, 4b, 5d, 6a

58–59
1. Insects, lizards,
   and plants
2. To help with digestion
3. For fighting
4. Plants

62–63
1. To take sharp turns
   and avoid obstacles
2. 20 in (50 cm)
3. Its club tail
4. Deinonychus

64–65
1d, 2c, 3a, 4b

70–71
True or False?
False

72–73
1. Page 81
2. Page 84
3. Page 84
4. Page 78
5. Page 88
6. Page 90
7. Page 81
8. Page 74
9. Page 77
10. Page 75
11. Page 87
12. Page 83

74–75
1b, 2b, 3a, 4b

78–79
True or False?
False

80–81
1b, 2d, 3a, 4c, 5e

84–85
1e, 2f, 3c, 4a, 5b, 6d

88–89
True or False?
False

Glossary

armor
Hard layer that covers the body of an animal and provides protection

asteroid
Rocky object that moves around the sun

battering ram
Ancient weapon with a metal knob in the front. It was used to break down walls or gates

bony plate
Pointy plates made of a bony material that were often found on a dinosaur's neck and back

carnivore
Animal that only eats other animals

climate
Weather of a particular place over a period of time

club
Weapon with a thick end used to fight enemies

conifer
Type of tree that produces cones and has needle-like leaves

continent
Large and continuous landmass. There are seven continents in the world

defense
Act of resisting an attack

digestion
Process of breaking down food into the chemical substances that your body needs to function

excavation
Digging the ground to remove and find things from the past

extinct
When an entire species no longer exists

ferns
Type of plant with feathery leaves found mainly in tropical areas

flipper
Flat limb belonging to an animal that lives underwater. It is used for swimming

fossil
Remains or traces of an ancient animal or plant, usually preserved in rock

fossilization
Process by which parts of an organism become fossils

frill
Protective shield around the necks of some dinosaurs. These could have spikes or be brightly colored

habitat
Animal's or plant's
natural environment

herbivore
Animal that only
eats plants

herd
Large group of the
same type of animal
that lives or travels
together

mammal
Warm-blooded animal
that feeds milk to its
young. Its body is
covered in hair

mass extinction
Disastrous event
that leads to the
disappearance of
living things in
large numbers

omnivore
Animal that eats
both plants and
other animals

paleontologist
Scientist who discovers
the history of life on the
planet by studying fossils

predator
Animal that kills
and eats other animals

prehistoric
Period of time before
written records were made

preserved
Animal, plant, or object that
has not changed much from
its original state of death
over a long period of time

prey
Animal that is killed
by other animals for food

scales
Tiny, overlapping
flat pieces of skin
on fish and reptiles

scavenger
Animal that eats
the remains of
other dead animals

shield
Object that provides
protection from harm

snout
Long, outward nose
found on animals,
such as dogs and rats

spikes
Pointy ends that
are long and narrow.
Some animals have
spike-shaped horns

weapon
Tool used to
fight an enemy

whip
Long and thin object
used to cause harm
to someone

Acknowledgments

Original edition: Design Charlotte Bull, Glenda Fisher, Elaine Hewson, Ria Holland, Charlotte Johnson, Clare Shedden, Yumiko Tahata; **Editorial** James Mitchem, Ellie de Rose; **Illustration** Helen Dodsworth, Chris Howker, Barney Ibbotson, Jake McDonald; Consultant Darren Naish

DORLING KINDERSLEY would like to thank: Rea Pikula for proofreading; Gunjan Mewati for editorial support.

The publisher would like to thank the following for their kind permission to reproduce their photographs:

(Key: a-above; b-below/bottom; c-center; f-far; l-left; r-right; t-top)

1 Dreamstime.com: Daniel Eskridge (clb). **2–3 Dreamstime.com:** Daboost. **4 123RF.com:** Oleksiy (tr). **Dreamstime.com:** Robyn Mackenzie / Robynmac (t). **6 Dreamstime.com:** Anastasiya Aheyeva (bl); Linda Bucklin (tr). **7 Getty Images:** Science Photo Library / Mark Garlick (clb). **8 Dreamstime.com:** Linda Bucklin (cra); Elena Duvernay (clb). **9 Dreamstime.com:** Mr1805 (clb). **16 Dorling Kindersley:** Jon Hughes (cra). **Dreamstime.com:** Corey A Ford (ca). **16–17 Dreamstime.com:** Ensuper. **17 Dorling Kindersley:** Jon Hughes (br); Natural History Museum, London (ca). **19 Dorling Kindersley:** Jon Hughes (ca). **20–21 Dreamstime.com:** Leonello Calvetti (Allosaurus); Daniel Eskridge (ca); Corey A Ford (Ceratosaurus, Coelophysis). **20 123RF.com:** Leonello Calvetti (Allosaurus). **Dreamstime.com:** Corey A Ford (br); Sofia Santos (br/cra). **21 123RF.com:** Michael Rosskothen (x3). **Dreamstime.com:** Daniel Eskridge (br). **22 Getty Images:** Science Photo Library / Mark Garlick (cr). **23 Dorling Kindersley:** Dan Crisp (ca). **24–25 Dreamstime.com:** Anastasiya Aheyeva. **25 Dreamstime.com:** Antoniosantosg (ca). **27 Dreamstime.com:** Corey A Ford (cl); Jianghongyan (br). **30 Dorling Kindersley:** Jon Hughes (clb); Peter Minister, Digital Sculptor (br). **Fotolia:** DM7 (tl). **31 123RF.com:** Mark Turner (cl). **Dorling Kindersley:** Andy Crawford / Robert L. Braun (tl); Jon Hughes (tr). **32 Dorling Kindersley:** Jon Hughes (clb). **32–33 Dorling Kindersley:** Gary Ombler / Robert L. Braun (x3). **33 Dorling Kindersley:** Roby Braun / Gary Ombler (tc); Jon Hughes (cla). **34 Dorling Kindersley:** Jon Hughes (bl). **35 Dorling Kindersley:** Jon Hughes (l); Gary Ombler / Robert L. Braun (ca). **36 Dreamstime.com:** Mr1805 (cla). **37 Getty Images / iStock:** Racksuz (c). **39 Dreamstime.com:** Stevesg (tl). **40 123RF.com:** Mark Turner (bl). **Dorling Kindersley:** Peter Minister, Digital Sculptor (cb). **41 123RF.com:** Mark Turner (tc). **Dorling Kindersley:** Peter Minister, Digital Sculptor (cb); Gary Ombler / Robert L. Braun (tr). **42 Dorling Kindersley:** Andy Crawford / Robert L. Braun (cl, bc, cla, cra); Jon Hughes (x2). **Fotolia:** DM7 (bl, cla). **43 Dorling Kindersley:** Andy Crawford / Robert L. Braun (x8); Jon Hughes (cr). **Fotolia:** DM7 (cb/x2). **46 Dorling Kindersley:** Natural History Museum, London (bl). **Getty Images / iStock:** Damian Lugowski (clb). **47 Dorling Kindersley:** James Kuether (br). **Dreamstime.com:** Akarakingdoms (cr). **50 Dorling Kindersley:** Jon Hughes (br); Natural History Museum, London (bl). **52–53 123RF.com:** Mark Turner (x5). **56–57 Dreamstime.com:** Luchschen (ca). **56 Dorling Kindersley:** Jon Hughes (bl); Natural History Museum, London (br). **Dreamstime.com:** Sang Lei (t). **57 Dorling Kindersley:** Andy Crawford / Robert L. Braun (br).

Dreamstime.com: Cristina Bernhardsen (tr). **Getty Images / iStock:** Damian Lugowski (crb). **58 Alamy Stock Photo:** Stocktrek Images, Inc. / Nobumichi Tamura (cl). **59 Dorling Kindersley:** Dynamo (cl). **62 Dorling Kindersley:** James Kuether (br). **62–63 Depositphotos Inc:** adekvat (rocks). **64–65 Dreamstime.com:** Leelloo. **65 Alamy Stock Photo:** Xinhua (t). **66 Alamy Stock Photo:** Stocktrek Images, Inc. / Nobumichi Tamura (b). **Dreamstime.com:** Christophe Testi (cl). **66–67 Dreamstime.com:** Sataporn Jiwjalaen / Onairjiw. **67 Alamy Stock Photo:** Mohamad Haghani (bl). **69 Dorling Kindersley:** Jerry Young (cra). **70 Dreamstime.com:** Akarakingdoms (t); Alexstar (cl). **71 Dreamstime.com:** Akarakingdoms (t); Leonello Calvetti (bc). **72 Dorling Kindersley:** Jon Hughes (clb); Natural History Museum (bl). **73 Dorling Kindersley:** Jon Hughes (crb); Royal Tyrrell Museum of Palaeontology, Alberta, Canada (bl). **74 Dorling Kindersley:** Natural History Museum, London (bl). **Dreamstime.com:** Leonello Calvetti (bc). **75 Alamy Stock Photo:** Stocktrek Images, Inc. / Sergey Krasovskiy (cl). **Dorling Kindersley:** Jon Hughes (br). **80 Dreamstime.com:** Mr1805 (ca). **81 Dreamstime.com:** Mark Turner (ca). **82 Dreamstime.com:** Christophe Testi (bl). **83 Dorling Kindersley:** Andy Crawford / Roby Braun (bc, tr). **84 Dorling Kindersley:** Jon Hughes (crb, clb, tr, bc, bl). **87 Dorling Kindersley:** American Museum of Natural History (ca); Royal Tyrrell Museum of Palaeontology, Alberta, Canada (cra). **88 Alamy Stock Photo:** Natural History Museum, London (br). **Dorling Kindersley:** Natural History Museum (bl). **Getty Images / iStock:** CoreyFord (c). **88–89 Dreamstime.com:** Linda Bucklin (c). **89 Dorling Kindersley:** Senckenberg Nature Museum (br). **Dreamstime.com:** Jakekohlberg (bl). **92 Dorling Kindersley:** Peter Minister, Digital Sculptor (cl). **Dreamstime.com:** Alexstar (cl/glass). **94 Dorling Kindersley:** Gary Ombler / Robert L. Braun (tc); Royal Tyrrell Museum of Palaeontology, Alberta, Canada (br). **Dreamstime.com:** Christophe Testi (tc/pencil). **95 Getty Images:** Science Photo Library / Mark Garlick

Cover images: *Front:* **Dorling Kindersley:** Andy Crawford / Robert L. Braun cla, Jon Hughes crb, Peter Minister cl; *Back:* **Dorling Kindersley:** Jon Hughes cr, Royal Tyrrell Museum of Palaeontology, Alberta, Canada cra

All other images © Dorling Kindersley